The God of Our Deepest Longings

The God of Our Deepest Longings

Seven Biblical Meditations

Peter van Breemen, S.J.

Translated from German by Peter Heinegg

ave maria press AmP notre dame, indiana

Translation © 2009 by Ave Maria Press, Inc.

Founded in 1865, Ave Maria Press is a ministry of the Indiana Province of Holy Cross.

www.avemariapress.com

ISBN-10 1-59471-200-X ISBN-13 978-1-59471-200-5

Cover design by Brian C. Conley.

Cover Image: Photos.com

Printed and bound in the United States of America.

Library of Congress Cataloging-in-Publication Data is available.

Van Breemen, Peter G., 1927-
    [Im Geheimnis daheim. English]
    The God of our deepest longings : seven biblical meditations / Peter G. van Breemen ; translated from German by Peter Heinegg.
        p. cm.
    ISBN-13: 978-1-59471-200-5
    ISBN-10: 1-59471-200-X
    1. Meditations. 2. Bible--Meditations. 3. Spiritual life--Catholic Church.
I. Title.

    BX2182.3.V3413 2009
    242'.5--dc22
                                        2008047670

CONTENTS

Introduction

P roblems are to be solved, at least to the best of our ability. Mysteries, on the other hand, are to be respected—lived with, perhaps even inhabited. As human persons we are in many ways problematic. Yet at the same time we are also deeply mysterious. Science tries to solve our human problems, often with amazing success. Mystery, however, is not solvable. Contemplation, on the contrary, opens us up to the inexhaustible Mystery in order to find in it acceptance and strength, wisdom and hope, and, yes, even a home in it. The mystery of the human person is completely rooted in the mystery of God, who is more intimate to us than we are to ourselves and who at the same time transcends us immensely. This implies both a gift and a challenge.

The seven biblical meditations in this book circle around the mystery of God living in us and enabling us to become who we are. They are meant to assist readers in prayerfully opening themselves to the mystery of God, who is always revealing and addressing himself to us in Jesus Christ, and thus to shape their personal and communal lives truthfully and fruitfully.

ONE

What Are You Looking For?

The first words that Jesus speaks in each of the four Gospels have a special resonance and set the tone for the whole Gospel. In John the first statement made by Jesus neither proclaims, reveals, nor commands, but poses a question. The question takes those addressed as its point of departure and puts them in the center: "What are you looking for?" (Jn 1:38). This question is the first of a total of forty-four questions that Jesus asks in the fourth gospel. It articulates a pastoral approach that takes others seriously and challenges them to take themselves seriously. It is striking that in John the first words by the risen Lord are a variation on the same question: "Whom are you looking for?" (Jn 20:15; cf. also 18:4–7). It is *the* question for the Johannine Jesus. He invites us to become aware of our desires and to express them to him in our own words.

A child has the privilege of being allowed to make its wishes known. No normal child needs to be told that. If I were to come into a family where the children didn't express their wishes, I would feel ill at ease; either the children were inhibited or the parents were far too strict. As children of God, we are all encouraged to bring our wishes and our longings before God in prayer. "Ask, and it will be given you; search, and you will find; knock, and the door will be opened for you. . . . If you then, who are evil, know how to give good gifts to your children, how much more will your Father in heaven give good things to those who ask him!" (Mt 7:7, 11). Inspired by this invitation Saint Ignatius of Loyola recommended to retreatants that at the beginning of every prayer session they ask for what they desire. Accordingly, the most frequently met with phrase in his *Spiritual Exercises* is: "To ask what I want" (e.g., *Sp Ex* 48). Ignatius knows that every person is a pent up mass of longings and that this shapes our life, both when we get what we want and when we don't. "We choose our joys and our sorrows, long before we experience [them]," Kahlil Gibran has written.

However, anyone who tries to express his or her deepest longing will soon notice that this isn't easy. Precisely because our happiness in life is so very much dependent upon it, we usually keep our longing so carefully stored away that we can hardly bring it to light. It is hidden away in a realm where our understanding has a hard time gaining access. The English philosopher Ernest Gellner compares human intelligence to the publicity department of a large, complicated, and somewhat turbulent corporation run by a secretive and internally divided board of directors. The latter take good care to prevent the PR people from ever getting a clear picture of what management is up to. Yet it is the PR people who do the talking. In a famous pun Blaise Pascal (1623–1662) says it succinctly, "The heart has its reasons that reason knows nothing about" (*Pensées*, 277).

We often lack a sufficient awareness to recognize our deepest longing and take it seriously, much less to verbalize it. With his first words in the Gospel of John, Jesus invites us to do just that. To accept the invitation is a first step on the path into the Mystery in which we have our roots. The oft-used word "spirituality" basically refers to what we do with our longing, both in the fulfillment we experience when it materializes, as well as in the pain we feel when it doesn't. Spirituality above all confronts us with the basic question: How much does our longing coincide with the will of God?

Another difficulty comes from the fact that the word "longing" is often used inauthentically in two different ways. On the one hand, people speak of longing, when in reality there is nothing more than a weak "I'd like to," without the will or the effort to actually turn what they wish into reality. On the other hand, the word longing is occasionally used in a veiled sense, where what is really meant is a demand, and where non-fulfillment is felt to be a rejection. Real longing, by contrast, is energetic and ready for action, but at the same time open and receptive.

Our longings undoubtedly form a palette of very different and, to some extent, contradictory wishes. We find too that these longings are not all equally important, and we do not desire everything with the same intensity. Behind many a wish lies another, more significant one. In her book *Inner Compass* Margaret Silf tells the story of a little a girl who absolutely had to have a puppy and a bicycle. She expressed her wishes unmistakably. In fact she got the one for her birthday and the other for Christmas and at first she was perfectly satisfied. But it didn't last long. Soon she became restless and discontented once again. As a grown woman she realized that behind the wish for a dog lay a feeling of loneliness, and behind the bicycle a need for mobility

If it is hard to decipher one's own deeper desires, how much more difficult is it for our spouse, friend, or companion to know what we really want. How often relations between people lead to disappointments because they have mistaken ideas of what the other person wants. It is pretty obvious that the other person cannot, with any certainty, know what you desire unless you tell him or her.

Thus we ineluctably come to the question: What is our genuine and deep longing? The answer we give this question is important, because it is in this deepest longing that we can recognize God's will. But it is also hard, because we have hardly any access to this level of our own hearts. A Jesuit novice master related that he saw his greatest challenge as helping his men to become free enough to hear what their hearts really long for. There is so much noise, pressure, group compulsion, rivalry, and control by outsiders that the requisite freedom can be achieved only with difficulty. They must be liberated into their deepest desires.

As a retreat director, one of the most grati-
fying experiences is to see how a retreatant
reaches a level of stillness where his or her
desires become clear. Many times retreatants
have shared with me at the beginning of a
retreat some difficult dilemma they are in or a
serious problem they have to tackle. After lis-
tening both with my ears and my heart, I usually advise them to put the problem on the
shelf for the time being and just to take their
time with entering into the silence of the retreat
without being bothered by their burning question, as far as possible. And even though it may
pop up many times, I suggest that each time
they commend it into the Father's hands, as
Jesus did on the cross (cf. Lk 23:46). Once the
retreatants have reached that "center of stillness, surrounded by silence" (as Dag
Hammerskjöld calls it), they usually get a different perspective, which sometimes reveals
the answer to them clearly and effortlessly. I
have repeatedly witnessed the consolation of
that experience and partaken in its joy.

> We won't reach this level of profound con-
> sciousness so long as we just grind away or
> exert pressure on ourselves. Instead, we have
> to get rid of the dirt and mud to expose the
> bedrock that supports our life, or—switching
> images—to lay bare the wellspring that lets

living water gush forth. Saint Paul says: "For to me, living is Christ and dying is gain" (Phil 1:21). What would we call "living"? There's a line from a song that says, "Your deepest longing gives you the best advice." What does this phrase trigger in us? Or maybe the reverse way of approaching helps: We ask ourselves what irritates us, what we're afraid of, what resistances we sense. The heart of the matter is always that we must move past our superficial wishes in order to become internally free enough to listen to our deepest longings. "For where your treasure is, there your heart will be also," says Jesus in the Sermon on the Mount (Mt 6:21). How can we discover this treasure?

For Ignatius our deepest longing is identical with the will of God. To his mind this was crucial. Of the approximately seven thousand letters he wrote that have been preserved, 993 close with something like this request: "to God's infinite goodness, that he may give us the perfect grace to recognize his most holy will and perfectly accomplish it." Ignatius was convinced that we must find this will of God in our own hearts.

The French Jesuit Jean-Claude Guy (1927–1986), a specialist in the history of spirituality, in particular Jesuit spirituality, used to tell a parable that presents Ignatius's approach in a clear and somewhat provocative light. The imaginary story occurs in Rome at the time when Ignatius was superior general of the young Jesuit order. By this time several colleges were already being run by the Fathers. Two of these institutions had an urgent need for an extra Jesuit to take care of business. One college was in Venice, where the Order was beloved and honored by the people; the other was in Naples, where the brethren were despised and defamed on all sides, and their life and work had become extremely wearisome. Both colleges announced their needs to the General and begged him to send them someone, but Ignatius had only one candidate available. How could he determine where this one member of the Order should be assigned in keeping with God's will?

How would a present-day superior address this question? Undoubtedly, he would have a long talk with the person in question and take counsel with some people who know him or perhaps even call in an expert. He would try to size up the character, the psychic "carrying capacity," and the religious depth of the man. He would bring everything before God in prayer and in this way carefully grope toward a solution.

Ignatius had a different method. He was convinced that the answer could only be found in the heart of the candidate himself. So he called the candidate in and said that he planned to send him to one of the two colleges. He then described exactly the situation in the two cities. Before the Jesuit could spontaneously realize which of the two colleges he felt more drawn to, Ignatius sent him off to the chapel to pray for three hours, asking God for inner freedom before the two possibilities. Ignatius calls that "holy indifference": the attitude of heartfelt readiness to accept either alternative. When after three hours the Jesuit returned to him, Ignatius asked him whether he had really relinquished his own will. The candidate replied that he sincerely thought that in this matter he was inwardly free of his own wishes. Then Ignatius said to him: "And now tell me what you really want?" And that settled it. The saint's secretary commented: "Ignatius knew that the desire which remains in the heart, once someone had completely renounced his own will, coincides precisely with the will of God for this person."

For Ignatius, a decision according to God's will never depends solely on organizational emergencies or other external circumstances. He would never use a person just to fill a gap.

The situation and the facts of the case naturally play an important role, but only as they play out in the depths of the heart of the person concerned. For Ignatius, tremendous honesty in a state of inner freedom—holy indifference—constitutes the foundation of obedience.

And on this point Ignatius by no means stood alone. Saint John of the Cross (1542–1591) writes in the same sixteenth century: "Renounce your wishes, and you will discover what your heart really desires. Otherwise, how can you know whether your wishes correspond to God's will? Give up on your longings, and you will find what your heart yearns for. How do you know whether what you strive for is what God has in mind?"

About a hundred years later Blaise Pascal says in the prayer "You alone":

> Everything that is not you, God,
> cannot fulfill my hopes.
> God, I seek and desire you yourself.
> To you alone, my God, I turn.
> You alone could create my soul,
> you alone can create it anew.
> You alone could stamp it with your image,
> you alone can stamp it anew
> and impress your countenance on it again,
> which is Jesus Christ, my Savior,
> who is your image and the sign of your being.

The God of Our Deepest Longings

If we could all realize our most authentic longings, then the kingdom of God would be here. The will of God isn't something strange and terrible that gets laid down on top of us and to which we must blindly bow. On the contrary, it corresponds to our true deepest being. "The word of God is the opponent of your will until it becomes the author of your salvation. So long as you are your own enemy, the word of God is your enemy as well. Be your own friend; then the word of God will also be in harmony with you," Augustine teaches us.

Just as, on the level of being, God is the deepest foundation of our nature—nearer to ourselves than we ourselves—so in the realm of the will, God's will is identical to our own deepest personal will. "My Father is glorified by this, that you bear much fruit and become my disciples" (Jn 15:8). God wants to see the unfolding and true fulfillment of our person—much more than we ourselves want to. This creates a challenging and vital tension in our lives. "I came that they may have life, and have it abundantly" (Jn 10:10). God's will for us to live is stronger and more authentic than our own. In the silence of our hearts we can come into contact with this divine will to live life to the fullest.

The Psalmist advises us: "Take delight in the LORD, and he will give you the desires of your heart" (Ps 37:4). Perhaps someone might like to reverse that order: first, get what your heart desires, and then warmly rejoice in the Lord. But then the serious question arises whether one is really rejoicing in the Lord or rather in the Lord's gifts; they're not the same. The prophet Habakkuk prays:

> Though the fig tree does not blossom,
> and no fruit is on the vines;
> though the produce of the olive fails
> and the fields yield no food;
> though the flock is cut off from the fold
> and there is no herd in the stalls,
> yet will I rejoice in the LORD;
> I will exult in the God of my salvation.
>
> —HABAKKUK 3:17–18

With this attitude a person selflessly rejoices in God. He or she will experience how God fulfills the deepest longings of one's heart. Jesus teaches us this same truth in a parable: "The kingdom of heaven is like treasure hidden in a field, which someone found and hid; then in his joy he goes and sells all that he has and buys that field" (Mt 13:44). First comes joy in God. This makes us free enough to surrender everything, and in so doing to experience the fulfillment of our deepest longing: a peace that the world cannot give (cf. Jn 14:27).

G od,

You are the deepest ground of our being

and you love us infinitely more than we love ourselves.

Help us to open ourselves up

to your life-giving and challenging presence in us.

Enlighten the eyes of our heart

to discern your most holy will,

in which all that is good

has its source and sustenance,

today and every day, for ever and ever.

S U M M A R Y

Encountering God is primarily a matter of the heart, though no doubt the intellect also plays a role. "Blessed are the pure in heart, for they will see God" (Mt 5:8). Our deepest and most authentic desire is the point at which we are most united with God. It requires a great sincerity and inner freedom to identify that desire.

John 1:38

1 Kings 3:5

Mark 10:46-52

Philippians 2:13

```
┌─────────────────────────────────────────┐
│                                           │
│                                           │
│                                           │
│   Q U E S T I O N S   F O R   R E F L E C T I O N   │
└─────────────────────────────────────────┘
```

1. What do I recognize now as my deepest
    desire?

2. What do I dislike most?

3. What do I fear most?

4. What prevents me most from being com-
    pletely open to God's will?

5. Have I ever experienced the consolation
    of discovering my deepest longing?

Where Do You Live?

ndrew and John, Jesus' disciples, answer the question, "What are you looking for?" with a counter-question: "Rabbi" (John adds, "which translated means Teacher"), "where are you staying?" (Jn 1:38). As often in John's gospel, this counter-question plays out on two different levels. First, the disciples are inquiring quite literally about the whereabouts, the house, or, as Martin Luther translated it, the lodging of Jesus. In another way the question refers to Jesus' roots, to his place of origin; and the evangelist is, of course, thinking of his origin in the Father. Later Jesus will say: ". . . so that you may know and understand that the Father is in me and I am in the Father" (Jn 10:38). What is at stake here is

Jesus' deepest mystery, his essential unity with the Father, which John in particular keeps stressing.

We pray with the Psalmist: "How lovely is your dwelling place, O LORD of hosts! My soul longs, indeed it faints for the courts of the LORD. . . . For a day in your courts is better than a thousand elsewhere. I would rather be door-keeper in the house of my God than live in the tents of wickedness" (Ps 84:1–10). In the New Testament, Jesus reveals that he himself is this temple: "'Destroy this temple, and in three days I will raise it up'. . . . But he was speaking of the temple of his body" (Jn 2:19–21). The Father dwells in him and he dwells in the Father. That's what the disciples are asking about, without fathoming the depth of their own question.

The word "dwell" or "stay" or "abide" (in Greek, *menein*) is one of John's favorite words. It occurs forty times in his gospel and twenty-seven times in the letters attributed to him. In most cases the spatial sense is secondary; the word becomes an image for security and even unity. One may—and must—dwell in mysteries as in a home. In German the word for "mystery" (*Geheimnis*) has an echo of "home" (*Heim*) in it. Pity the person who has no mysteries or secrets; he or she is, as it were, spiritually or emotionally homeless. It is important that one lavishes care and attention on mysteries. We have many problems in our lives and we have to solve them as best we can. But there are also mysteries. These are insolvable, and under no circumstance can or should one solve them. They are enormously precious. It is a fatal mistake not to distinguish between problems and mysteries. Thus, for example, the Eucharist is not a problem at all, but an exceedingly rich mystery—one we can live on.

Everyone longs for security, for a home, for one's roots. People who don't find this security cannot become who they really are, and will never know true peace. Many individuals are burdened with a severe problem because at the beginning of their lives they were given too little of this security. Rejection comes in many forms. There is the unloved child who never experienced acceptance in his parents' house. Raised in an atmosphere of constant rejection, he or she will reject others too, and is likely to become highly anxious or quarrelsome. All their lives such people may feel themselves to be a burden for others. There are successful individuals who even in the second half of their lives have to continuously prove their worth, to the point of morbid ambition, and who never learn to handle failure.

By using the word "dwell" so often, John is expressing, first of all, the inner unity between Jesus and his Father. Jesus is "at home" in his Father, and always united with him. "The Father and I are one" (Jn 10:30). Here is the source of the ease displayed by Jesus, letting him deal with the most varied sorts of people in a liberating fashion, free from all anxiety. He was afraid of neither a leper nor the high priest, neither an adulteress nor the Roman governor. In his outgoing way, he was never superficial nor egocentric, but sincerely and lovingly oriented to others. When necessary, he didn't shy away from conflict or confrontation; but he always remained objective and fair. He maintained an inner calm because he was always rooted in his Father and lived from that source. "The one who sent me is with me; he has not left me alone, for I always do what is pleasing to him" (Jn 8:29). Jesus lived in a state of security that greatly transcends our experience and understanding, and that is what the Johannine term "dwelling" repeatedly points to.

Nevertheless, in the Gospel of John, "dwelling" doesn't refer only to the unity of Jesus with the Father, but in many cases to the relationship between Jesus and his disciples. On Easter morning he sends Mary Magdalene to his disciples with the message: "I am ascending to my Father and your Father, to my God and your God" (Jn 20:17). In these words Jesus sums up the fulfillment of his mission. He has come so that *his* Father may become *our* Father, and so that we may be at home with him in the mystery in which he himself is rooted and grounded. In this sense he prays in his high priestly prayer for all those who believe in him through the word of his disciples: ". . . that they may all be one. As you, Father, are in me and I am in you, may they also be in us, so that the world may believe that you have sent me. The glory that you have given me I have given them, so that they may be one, as we are one, I in them and you in me, that they may become completely one" (Jn 17:21–23). We are no longer slaves who always have to be afraid, but we have received the Spirit, in whom the Father and Son are perfectly one and in whom we too, as children of God, may call out as Jesus did, "Abba, Father" (cf. Rom 8:15–16).

Jesus assures us that, "In my Father's house there are many dwelling places" (Jn 14:2). There everyone's individuality will be respected and come fully into play. The unity based on God leaves room for great variety; in fact it promotes it. True unity is never anything like monotony: "On that day you will know that I am in the Father, and you in me, and I in you" (Jn 14:20). Jesus' dwelling within us and our dwelling within him both rest on Jesus' unity with the Father. Here too it is obviously not a question of physical space. What is meant is rather the union of life and love. We are the branches, in which the sap, the vital power of the vine, is present and effective and fruitful. We can love our unique fellow men and women because Jesus, with all his capacity for love, is in us. "Abide in me as I abide in you" (Jn 15:4). "As the Father has loved me, so I have loved you; abide in my love" (Jn 15:9). Lifted up and transformed in Jesus and in his and our Father, our life can unfold in all the fullness that God has planned for us. He, the God of Israel, has granted us "that we, being rescued from the hands of our enemies, might serve him without fear, in holiness and right-eousness before him all our days" (Lk 1:74–75).

This abiding in Jesus and in his Father is not static, but contains an enormous dynamism. God is always greater. However grand our thoughts about him may be, he is still grander. And if we actually do think grander thoughts about him, he is still greater than that. Thus, we constantly remain on our way, but behind him. Ignatius often called himself a "pilgrim," not just because he went

The God of Our Deepest Longings

on so many pilgrimages "alone and on foot," but because he always remained en route to the ever greater God with whom he could never quite catch up. Thus, the following of Christ is a continuous being-on-the-way, in the course of which we keep having to let go, in order to be able to enter untrodden territory. "So therefore, none of you can become my disciple if you do not give up all your possessions" (Lk 14:33).

To the question by the two disciples of where Jesus was staying, he answers, "Come and see" (Jn 1:39). Come, with your whole person, just as you are, with your strengths and your weaknesses, with your ideals and your disappointments. Commit yourself completely to the encounter. Don't send an artificial personality to search for God; come as you are, so that you can become what you were meant to be. The person is the question, God is the answer. Don't play a role, but dare to be authentic vis-à-vis Jesus. The truth will set you free, and in Jesus you will encounter the truth (cf. Jn 8:32–36). "He brought me out into a broad place; he delivered me, because he delighted in me" (Ps 18:20). You are heartily welcome, because he came for you. He wants you in your uniqueness, which he will deepen and purify.

And see! The disciples stayed with him all day. They looked and wondered. For the rest of their lives they could never forget this meeting. It changed their lives from the bottom up, and expanded their hearts. All of John's gospel is an invitation to do one thing: to come and see. In this gazing, in contemplation, a person is transformed. John experienced it personally, and in the opening verses of his first letter, this moving experience clearly reverberates: "We declare to you what was from the beginning, what we have heard, what we have seen with our eyes, what we have looked at and touched with our hands, concerning the word of life— this life was revealed, and we have seen it and testify to it, and declare to you the eternal life that was with the Father and was revealed to us" (1 Jn 1:1–2).

If we recognize Jesus' self-revelation, we recognize ourselves at the same time. *"Noverim te, noverim me,"* prays Saint Augustine, "May I come to know you, may I come to know myself." In Jesus we find God and hence ourselves in a new truthfulness. Meeting Jesus in prayer transforms a person. That's the secret of Ignatius' *Spiritual Exercises*.

When directing retreats I always invite the group to an hour of adoration of the Blessed Sacrament in the evening. Many retreatants tell me that this turns out to be a powerful experience for them. Jesus shows himself to us; we show ourselves to him. There is an intensity of presence that helps focus and renews us. I remember a Protestant woman who made a thirty-day retreat. At the beginning of the month she felt uncomfortable in joining the group for this hour. I left her completely free, of course, and respected her hesitation. She did keep coming, though, and discovered a hitherto unknown dimension of the Holy Eucharist. One or two years after the retreat was over she surprised me with a small book in which eight Protestant authors witness of their experiences with Holy Communion. She was one of them, and described in warm words what these nightly hours of eucharistic adoration had done to her. Needless to say I was very happy with her contribution.

Saint Paul expresses the effectiveness of contemplation in a dense statement, as follows: "And all of us, with unveiled faces, seeing the glory of the Lord as though reflected in a mirror, are being transformed into the same image from one degree of glory to another; for this comes from the Lord, the Spirit" (2 Cor 3:18). The transformation into the image of Jesus takes place, not thanks to our own strength and effort, but to the Spirit of the Lord, who

accomplishes it in us. In most cases this transformation remains hidden for a long time, even
from ourselves. It occurs at the deepest level of
our being, so far down that we ourselves have
no direct access to it; and it makes its presence
felt in our thinking and behavior only after a
considerable time has passed.

Dear Jesus,

you want to lead us into the intimacy

in which you are one with the Father,

so that our lives are like yours, rooted and grounded

in the mystery of the Blessed Trinity:

the mystery of unconditional love and complete

self-giving.

Grant us the grace to truly make our home with you

in the unity of the Father and the Holy Spirit,

for ever and ever. Amen.

SUMMARY

The disciples inquire about the home of Jesus. The answer turns out to have an astonishing depth and reveals something of the intimate union between Jesus and his Father. We are all invited to make our home in the love which binds Father and Son in the Holy Spirit.

```
┌─────────────────────────────────────┐
│                                     │
│                                     │
│                                     │
│                                     │
│      S C R I P T U R E   P A S S A G E S      │
└─────────────────────────────────────┘
```

Psalm 84:1-5

John 14:1-3:23

John 17:20-23

Revelation 3:20

1. What do I consider as most meaningful in my life?

2. What is for me the strongest source of confidence and security?

3. What does it mean for me to live united with God, and what helps me most to this union?

4. How would I describe what the mystery of the Blessed Trinity means to me?

THREE

What Supports You?

"No human being has ever desired anything as much as God desires to be with him or her." With these simple words Meister Eckhart (1260–1328) expressed a basic truth of our Christian faith. We cannot imagine how much God desires each one of us. "Thou burning God in your longing," prays the German mystic Mechtild of Magdeburg (1207–1282), and she explains:

> God has enough of all things. Contact with the soul is the one thing he never has enough of. He says: "That I love you exceedingly is part of my nature, because I am love itself. That I love you often comes from my longing, because I long to be heartily loved.

That I love you for so long comes from my eternity, because I am without beginning and end."

It is inherent to God's nature that he wishes to give himself. The mystery of the Trinity is not so much that three are one, and are three; but rather that the Father can give himself so totally, that the whole fullness of the Father is in the Son, and that the Son is capable of surrendering himself so completely to the Father that he holds nothing back of himself. Through this absolute giving of self, Father and Son are one in the Holy Spirit. It is this perfect unity through self-giving which transcends all our understanding and will forever remain a blessed mystery. Around the year 200 Tertullian introduced the word "Trinity" into the theological vocabulary, and thereby did us a disservice by setting us off on the heels of a number-problem, whereas the Trinity is really a mystery of unimaginable love. That mystery is the total self-surrender of divine love, which utterly surpasses human concepts.

The divine Persons do not only want to give themselves to one another; the triune God also wants to give God's very self to us, which is precisely why God created us. This is the meaning of creation and of our own lives. Since God is love, a love that by its very nature wants to give itself, God needs me. God loved me into existence and continues to do so at every moment in order to share divine love with me. In the concluding meditation of the *Spiritual Exercises* Ignatius asks the exercitant to consider "How the Lord wishes to give himself to me as much as he can" (*Sp Ex* 234). Meister Eckhart stresses: "God never gives a gift, and never has given one, so that we may possess it and restrict ourselves to that. Rather all gifts that he has ever given on heaven and earth, he gave with one end in view: he himself is the gift."

In the Psalms we read: "By the word of the Lord the heavens were made, and all their host by the breath of his mouth." And again: "For he spoke, and it came to be; he commanded, and it stood firm" (Ps 33:6, 9). The Psalmist is seeking to express the sovereign ease with which God created the universe. The Hebrew verb *dabar*, when used in reference to a human person, means "speak." But when applied to God, it means "create." The idea is that God needs only to speak, and what he says *is*.

But we can never speak about God with only *one* word or in only *one* image. God is too big for our little human words and thoughts. We always need a second word to complete the first, and another image to break up the first.

But even then our language always falls short. Thus, in the case of the truth that God creates just through speaking, one might think that anything that cost so little could not be worth very much—which would be a complete misunderstanding. The Anglican theologian William Vanstone reports an event that enriches and deepens our idea of creation. Before the Second World War a young man suffered severe brain damage in an accident. Only an operation could save him, but up until then no such operation had ever been performed. An experienced surgeon offered to try it, in hopes of saving the young man's life, but also stating clearly that there was only a very rare chance that the surgery would be successful. The operation was extremely difficult and dangerous, as one small mistake would have fatal consequences. Medically speaking, the intervention was off the map. The operation lasted seven hours, with the surgeon's concentration stretched to the limit throughout—and it worked. Afterwards the surgeon was completely exhausted and had to be led away by the nurse like a blind man or a little boy. He had really given everything he had to save the patient's life. This too is an image of divine creation.

According to Isaiah, God says to Israel: "Because you are precious in my sight, and honored, and I love you, I give people in return for you, nations in exchange for your life" (Is 43:4). Later the prophet adds: "As the bridegroom rejoices over the bride, so shall your God rejoice over you" (Is 62:5). In the New Testament, God's promise is expanded to all nations; everyone can take these words in an altogether personal sense. Paul goes even further: "He who did not withhold his own Son, but gave him up for all of us, will he not with him also give us everything else?" (Rom 8:32). Every person receives God's self-gift. Saint Teresa of Avila challenges us to "recognize the truth that there is in ourselves something incomparably more precious than what we externally perceive." She was a woman with a healthy sense of self. She liked to quote a text in which God speaks: "O soul, seek yourself in me; and, soul, seek me in yourself. . . . Thou art my house and my dwelling, thou art my home for ever and ever." The experience of such nearness and loyalty by God supported Teresa, and made her life extraordinarily fruitful.

The crucial thing is to let such texts make their way into our heart of hearts and to savor them to the fullest, in the holy conviction that they are meant quite personally for every one of us. It is all about me! A young woman was home by herself channel-surfing until she got bored. Then she went through the house and saw an open Bible on a cabinet. She looked at it and read the verse: "The LORD loved him [Solomon], and sent a message by the prophet Nathan; so he named him Jedidiah, because of the LORD" (2 Sam 12:24–25). In the footnote she read that Jedidiah means "beloved of the LORD." This phrase struck her, and she experienced an inescapable sense that it referred to her. She became blissfully happy, and began dancing around the deserted apartment. This intense experience wound up shaping her entire life. When she was later confirmed, she chose "Jedidiah" as her confirmation name. Even today she makes a point of using it.

An essential element of the doctrine of creation is that every person is a "wanted child," willed and affirmed by God. This contains an undreamt-of source of encouragement for accepting ourselves. The first act of adoring God consists in accepting the fact that we come from God's hand. Edith Stein writes: "[Our] love is entirely directed to God, but in union with divine love the created spirit also embraces itself in recognition, in free and happy affirmation, of itself. Surrender to God is at the same time surrender to one's own God-loved Self and the whole Creation."

The Christians in the early Church were for the most part simple people. But they always had the message proclaimed to them: *"Agnosce, Christiane, dignitatem tuam,"* ("Recognize, O Christian, your worth"). God has brought us together so that we can live and proclaim the truth of his love, which is directed at all of us. That is the Church. God loves every one of us into existence. God's complete, undivided love goes forth to every one of us. We have to internalize this message and make it the foundation of our life. The central-European mystic Angelus Silesius (1624–1677), who had a special talent for expressing profound truths in warm and clear words, puts it this way: "There is still nothing here more beautiful than I am, because God, beauty itself, has fallen in love with me."

A teacher was talking about modern discoveries in history class: "Can anyone name something important that didn't exist fifty years ago?" she asked. A bright youngster in the first row raised his hand and exclaimed: "Me!" God's unbounded yes is given to each one of us in advance and remains inviolably valid. All of us can find in this yes strength to support our lives. In fact, no one can make another person feel inferior without the victim's cooperation.

I remember vividly a woman coming up to me after a talk on this topic. She was upset. With a tense face and making a fist, she lamented, "I believe that God is love and that God loves everybody." And then much louder: "But I am the one exception. Stop it!" It touched me deeply and I sensed the intense suffering of the woman. She badly needed help, perhaps psychotherapy, to become free and open enough to accept the gospel message. But she certainly articulated pointedly how much faith in God's love is a gift and a grace beyond our grasp.

In 1994, after almost thirty years in prison, Nelson Mandela became President of South Africa. He quoted in his inaugural address some lines by Marianne Williamson from which he had evidently drawn a great deal of strength: "You are a child of God. When you belittle yourself, that doesn't help the world. . . . We are born to manifest the glory of God that is in us. God's glory isn't just in a few of us. God's glory is in every person. When we let our light shine, we likewise give others permission to let their light shine. When we set ourselves free from our own fear, we also free others with our presence."

God has a passionate longing for us to commit ourselves to his love and to welcome it emphatically. It is always and everywhere part of the nature of love that it wants to be accepted, and it is disappointed when this fails to happen. That is all the more true of divine love: "Listen! I am standing at the door, knocking; if you hear my voice and open the door, I will come in to you and eat with you, and you with me" (Rev 3:20). A meal is here, as often in scripture, an image of intimacy. God greatly longs for this meal, but he respects our freedom. If someone doesn't open, he doesn't force himself on that person. But he also doesn't go away; he knocks again after a while. Thanks to this perseverance he has already won over many people. God is the power of free attraction.

But at the same time accepting God's gift of self also means surrendering to God. That's why the line of Revelation is so accurate: "I . . . with you, and you with me." Committing oneself to God's love is an enormous challenge. God accepts us as we are, not as we should be, and unconditionally to boot. In so doing he provides us the possibility of becoming who we can be. The potential that we have within us is unleashed. God exerts no compulsion; he attracts and encourages and thereby makes possible growth and development that, left to ourselves, we could never achieve. The self-acceptance that springs from the love of God isn't static, but dynamic and stimulating. Once people have internalized the truth that they are unconditionally loved by God, they'll no longer let themselves be intimidated and limited by the insistent messages of advertising or the ever-present group pressures. The truth sets us free.

It is no surprise that everyone has tendencies that resist the love of God. Evil, the Adversary, lives in us, as we learn from scripture and all of tradition. Among the good seed the enemy sows weeds, which grow together down into the roots of the wheat, so that they can't be ripped out without destroying the good kernels as well (cf. Mt 13:24–30). A part of the good seed falls among thorns, which grow more quickly and powerfully, and so stifle the good plants. Jesus interprets the thorns to mean "the cares and riches and pleasures of life" (cf. Lk 8:7, 14). Paul warns us that "Even Satan disguises himself as an angel of light" (2 Cor 11:14). Ignatius adopts this teaching and develops it (*Sp Ex* 332). The Evil One is very well acquainted with the language of scripture and the finer points of psychology. At first the inspirations of God, the whisperings of the Evil One, and our own imaginings look bafflingly alike. By the time it becomes clear what is really at stake, it is often too late, or at least a lot of damage has already been done. Illusions can be easily concealed and, at the same time, extremely stubborn. We need a careful discernment of spirits so that our receptivity to the self-giving love of God is not badly spoiled. For that reason it is appropriate and helpful when in the liturgy of the Easter Vigil we join together and publicly renounce Satan and all his malice and all his allurements. In so doing we express the foundation and core of this discernment of spirits.

Gracious God,

Your love puts no condition and knows no limits.

It embraces and envelops us totally,

like the air we breathe.

It is life-giving in the most profound sense of the word.

Grant us the grace

to believe with all our hearts.

May this faith shape and permeate our personalities

and may it bear rich fruit in self-acceptance

and love of our neighbor.

Let us so become living witnesses of your love and truth

and give you honor and glory.

We ask this through Jesus Christ, your Son and our Lord,

In whom all your love was revealed.

SUMMARY

God loves each of us into existence, every moment of our lives. This renders us worthy and lovable. It is a free gift from the very beginning of our existence. It is our task to respond to this basic grace of God. There are, however, both outside and inside us, strong voices and forces trying to block precisely this process.

Isaiah 43:1-7

Isaiah 49:15-16.

Zephaniah 3:14-17

Romans 8:28-39

Ephesians 3:14-19

1. How would I summarize briefly and in my own words the core of my faith?

2. Who helps me to be more open to God's love, and how does he or she do this?

3. What hinders me from believing whole-heartedly in God's love for me as I am?

4. How does this faith sustain me in the dark hours of my life?

Becoming Transparent

On several occasions the Gospel of John calls Jesus the "light of the world." Jesus himself affirms: "I am the light of the world" (Jn 8:12). In the Sermon on the Mount, however, he says just as directly to his disciples: "You are the light of the world" (Mt 5:14)—not as a promise or an order, but as a simple statement of fact. Of course, there's no contradiction between the two sayings. In fact, they belong closely together: *We* are the light of the world because *he* is. "For it is the God who said, 'Let light shine out of darkness,' who has shone in our hearts" (2 Cor 4:6). "The LORD is my light and my salvation; whom shall I fear?" (Ps 27:1).

The Fathers of the Church liked to compare the Church to the moon. Just as the moon has no light in itself, but receives all its light from the sun, so the Church has no light of its own, but receives all its light from Jesus, its sun. This image can be developed further if one reflects that while the sun always shines in its full brilliance, the moon in its dependency on the sun waxes and wanes in continuously changing phases. Something similar can be observed in the Church.

Jesus vividly and clearly illustrates this dependency with another image: He calls himself the vine and us the branches (Jn 15:1–8). The fruitfulness of the branches derives entirely from the vital power of the vine, whose sap works in the branches. The light that we radiate comes entirely from him who is the light of the world.

Every day after the celebration of the Eucharist, the Missionaries of Charity, the order founded by Mother Teresa, recite a prayer that expresses the essence of their spirituality. It was composed by Cardinal John Henry Newman:

> Dear Jesus,
> help us to spread your fragrance everywhere
> we go.

Flood our souls with your spirit and life.
Penetrate and possess our whole being
so utterly
that all our lives may be only a radiance of
yours.
Shine through us, and be so in us,
that every soul we come in contact with
may feel your presence in our soul.
Let them look up and see no longer us but only
Jesus!
Stay with us, and then we shall begin to shine as
you shine,
so to shine as to be a light to others;
the light O Jesus, will be all from you,
none of it will be ours;
it will be you, shining on others through us.

Thomas of Celano writes in his first biography of Saint Francis of Assisi: "Saint Francis filled the whole world with the gospel of Christ . . . by proclaiming everywhere the glad tidings of the kingdom of God. In doing so he made his whole body into a tongue, so as to edify his listeners by example not less than by word." This gave rise to one of the "little flowers" (*fioretti*), the charming tale of how Saint Francis once invited a brother to go with him into town to preach. They went together into the city, but Saint Francis kept on going until he came out on the other side and left the city behind. Then the brother objected, "But we were supposed to preach." To which Francis answered, "And so we did."

There is an enlightening story about a boy who went to church with his mother on a sunny day. He was enthusiastic about the colorful figures that the sun traced through the stained glass windows onto the floor and he excitedly asked his mother what this and that meant. She whispered that this was such and such a saint, and that was another. Some time afterwards in religion class the teacher asked if anyone knew what a saint was. "I do," the boy announced, "someone that the light shines through." Not a bad description!

Elisabeth Kübler-Ross takes the image one step further: "It is lovely that the windows display their colorful images when the sun shines radiantly through them, but it would be far more helpful if the images would glow in the dark. That's possible, but only if there is a very strong source of light shining inside the church."

We can be the light of the world only if we become transparent for the light of the Lord in us. A German spiritual author, Johannes Bours, poses the question of what a pure soul might be. He answers his own question in two ways. First: "I'd like to put it this way. It is a person who is totally undisguised, who is quite himself or herself, at one with his or her nature, so that the call of God, the beauty of God, can come through him or her, pure and uninterrupted. A pure soul is a lover, who in purity looks away from himself or herself." He then adds another answer as well: "But perhaps this too is a pure soul: a person who knows his or her brokenness, his or her shadow, his or her guilt, and has no other longing than to be looked on by God, in order to become whole." He concludes: "God takes joy in human beings who reflect his beauty. The prophet Zephaniah renders this as follows: 'The LORD, your God, is in your midst. . . . He will rejoice over you with gladness' (3:17)."

The crucial thing is the art of becoming completely open and receptive. The Protestant mystic Gerhard Tersteegen (1693–1769) has summed this up in a short verse:

> Ah, were my spirit as pure, as silent and white. As a blank sheet on which one may write. Soon would God's Son his lovely image ignite. Deep within me with his rays of light!

The most beautiful text that I know about Mary is by the English Jesuit poet, Gerard Manley Hopkins (1844–1889), in "The Blessed Virgin Mary Compared to the Air We Breathe":

Mary Immaculate . . . who
This one work has to do—
Let all God's glory through,
God's glory, which would go
Thro' her, and from her flow
Off, and no way but so.

Indeed, the *entire* glory of God passed through Mary, undiluted and intact. And that was possible because she was fully transparent, perfectly "permeable," indeed immaculately conceived. In this way, and only in this way, did the glory of God in its complete fullness come into our world, as the Word that became flesh through Mary.

For Jesus the world was flooded with the presence of his Father. He encountered the Father everywhere: in the birds of the air and in the flowers of the field, in the sun rising and the rain falling down, but above all in human beings in their exuberant diversity. Jesus encountered the Father not only through thinking, but intuitively and immediately; and this is what enriched and fulfilled Jesus' life. For Jesus the whole creation was transparently open to the Father, because Jesus himself was transparent for the Father. The first half of the prayer that he shared with us is wholly oriented to the Father: "Hallowed be thy name. Thy kingdom come. Thy will be done." His food was to do the will of his Father (cf. Jn 4:34). He lived on this and for this. The Father's bidding was the content of his life, which is why he found the Father in all of it.

Here we are touching a nerve of the glad tidings, one that is liberating and happiness-inducing. It is a question of being transparent for God. According to the gospel, the art and joy of life consist in *letting* God act in and through us. That way a great burden is lifted from our shoulders. To the extent that I understand the New Age movement, It is more about self-awareness than self-forgetfulness, more about self-discovery than self-sacrifice, more about self-development than selfless love for God and one's neighbor. Christianity places the emphasis elsewhere: "Come to me, all you that are weary and are carrying heavy burdens, and I will give you rest. Take my yoke upon you, and learn from me; for I am gentle and humble in heart, and you will find rest for your souls" (Mt 11:28–29). In the Near East, wagons and plows were mostly pulled by a pair of oxen (cf. Lk 14:19). This image represents our union with Jesus realistically and as a very close one. We are his yoke-mates and carry out our work in harmony with him. In so doing we have to constantly pay attention to him, just as he is always intent on us.

Jesus is supposed to have said to Saint Catherine of Siena: "Look after me, then I will look after you." That's an exchange that does us good. The same message is already present in the Sermon on the Mount: "Your heavenly Father knows that you need all these things. But strive first for the kingdom of God and his righteousness, and all these things will be given to you as well" (Mt 6:32–33). That's an attitude toward life that makes us happy and free.

We have all met people who are very much aware that they come in the name of the Lord of Hosts and who never forget the awful responsibility that goes with such a mission. They may still have some sort of humor, but even that is heavy and not quite unencumbered. On the other side we have also met people who are deeply spiritual, radiating in an unpretentious manner a contagious joy, confidence, and freedom. They show something of that complete joy which Jesus wants to give to his disciples (Jn 15:11; 16:24; 17:13). Julian of Norwich (1342–ca. 1416) was such a person. In her *Revelations of Divine Love,* she wrote: "It is God's will that we have heartfelt joy with him in our salvation. God wants us to find great comfort and strength in it, and to be completely and happily taken up with it by his grace.

For we are God's happiness and God finds endless enjoyment in us, and we shall in him, by his grace."

The glad tidings enrich us immensely. Our most important task consists in making good use of these gifts as well as in honoring and celebrating their "giftedness," that is, to see the gift in the given. When modern Christians are asked what holiness is, most of them answer by suggesting that one is supposed to *become* holy, while most likely adding that it is a tall order. The early Church spoke and thought differently: holiness is given to us in baptism right from the beginning. Saint Paul usually begins his letters with a greeting "to the saints," meaning simply the local Christians.

No doubt this holiness, which has been given in advance for free, has to develop further, and that is a lifelong task. But it nonetheless makes an important difference whether one has already received this holiness or still has to acquire it. Holiness isn't something that grows out of prayer; rather, we pray because we are holy. Holiness isn't the result of our love of neighbor; rather we love our neighbor because we are holy. Holiness isn't a gift awarded to us after a life of service; rather, we do our service because we are holy.

We have been given a tremendous trove of gifts. We are allowed to live as children of God. We are allowed to draw from an ever-flowing source: "With joy you will draw water from the wells of salvation" (Is 12:3). "For with you is the fountain of life; in your light we see light" (Ps 36:9). "Lo, everyone who thirsts, come to the waters; and you that have no money, come, buy and eat!" (Is 55:1).

In the New Testament Jesus reveals that he himself is this living water: "Let anyone who is thirsty come to me, and let the one who believes in me drink. As the scripture has said, 'Out of the believer's heart shall flow rivers of living water'" (Jn 7:37–38; cf. Jn 4:14). In the gospels Jesus shows himself through many signs to be the fullness of God. As early as his prologue, John announces: "From his fullness we have all received, grace upon grace" (Jn 1:16). Paul voices this wish for the saints in Ephesus: ". . . so that, with the eyes of your heart enlightened, you may know what is the hope to which he has called you, what are the riches of his glorious inheritance among the saints, and what is the immeasurable greatness of his power for us who believe" (Eph 1:18–19).

PRAYER

Jesus, you are

not a light-bearer, but light—the light;

not a signpost along the way, but the Way itself;

not a Truthful one, but Truth—the Truth;

not a Living one, but life—the Life;

not a great one, but Lord—the Lord.

In you we receive God's self-gift,

in complete fullness.

"To whom can we go?

You have the words of eternal life" (Jn 6:68).

SUMMARY

The secret of the Christian life is to let Jesus work in and through us. *His* light makes us the light of the world. The sap of the vine causes the branches to bear plenty of grapes. *His* holiness produces its fruits in *our* lives. Transparency is the key. In this way the glad tidings take a heavy burden from our shoulders and allow us to live joyfully and fruitfully as God's children.

```
┌─────────────────────────────────────────┐
│                                           │
│                                           │
│                                           │
│          S C R I P T U R E   P A S S A G E S │
└─────────────────────────────────────────┘
```

Isaiah 60:19-20

Ezekiel 47:1-12

John 15:1-11

Revelation 22:1-5

1. In what way do I experience the gospel as a heavy burden?

2. In what way is it for me life-giving and uplifting?

3. Do I know people who radiate the light of God, perhaps without even being conscious of it?

4. What does transparency mean for me?

5. What role does Mary play in my life?

FIVE

Living
from
Plenitude

Antoine de Saint-Exupéry (1900–1944) wrote a number of other books aside from his sublime *The Little Prince*. His main job was not as a writer, but as a pilot in France between the First and Second World Wars. He often flew over the Sahara, because France, his fatherland, had colonies in Africa at the time. On several occasions he had to make emergency landings in the desert. Once in an extreme emergency some Bedouins saved his life. In gratitude he invited three of these men to France. One could hardly imagine a greater culture shock. They had never seen a house, and now they suddenly landed in Paris with all its architectural treasures, its boulevards, its traffic, its Métro, and much else. Despite it all, however, they remained amazingly stolid. Finally their host surprised them with a tour in the Alps. There they came across a waterfall—a breath-taking experience for them. The water that plunged down it in a minute was enough to supply their entire tribe for a whole year, clear, fresh water which one could drink immediately. They could not get over their amazement and they refused to go on because they had witnessed a miracle. In their culture if they ever met with a miracle, they stayed by it as long as it lasted. There was nothing in the world that could persuade them to proceed further before the waterfall stopped. Indeed, Saint-Exupéry could not get them to move on, until in desperation he said, "But that has been flowing for a thousand years now!" Finally his guests believed him, and they continued their tour.

For me personally waterfalls have a great attraction, partly because in my home country there is plenty of water but not one waterfall. I was almost thirty when I saw my first one in Wales and it impressed me greatly. Many years later I met a Vietnamese priest who had studied both engineering and medicine in his native country before he had to flee. As one of the boat refugees, he was hijacked by pirates and eventually found a new home in the

United States. There he became a priest. He shared with me how waterfalls are very special to him. Where he grew up in Vietnam there were, unlike in my country, lots of them. "I used to spend plenty of time sitting beside them in fascination. One day my father, who was not a Christian, said to me: 'Waterfalls are like God, always the same and always new. We come to the waterfall every day and it is there always, but never the same water runs through it.' God is always there for us, constant and true, but God is always new too. And there is always that abundance."

So for me too the waterfall became a splendid image of the fullness that we are given in God. His love has been flowing for thousands of years and is a far greater wonder than what the Bedouins found in the Alps. The Carmelite saint Edith Stein writes: "Divine life is love, overflowing, lavish, freely self-giving love. Love that heals what is sick and awakens to life what is dead. Love that protects and cherishes, nourishes, grieves and is joyful with the joyous, that is helpful to every creature, so that it may become what the Father has destined it to be." There is a plenitude here that flows from and refers to the mystery of God. There is never a need to quarrel over anything. We all live on God's superfluity, whether we know it or not. But it is a great advantage to become aware of it in our hearts, because that gives life more solidity and brightness, more ease and coherence, and a greater inner freedom.

Jesus came in order to reveal this plenitude to us. Paul writes the pregnant sentence: "For in him [Jesus] the whole fullness of deity dwells bodily, and you have come to fullness in him" (Col 2:9–10). In Jesus we are fulfilled men and women. Paul prays "that Christ may dwell in your hearts through faith, as you are being rooted and grounded in love. I pray that you may have the power to comprehend, with all the saints, what is the breadth and length and height and depth, and to know the love of Christ that surpasses knowledge, so that you may be filled with all the fullness of God" (Eph 3:17–19). Jesus brings us life in plenitude (cf. Jn 10:10) and helps us so that it unfolds completely and brings rich fruit. He wants to make our joy complete.

In his old age, Simeon experienced in the child Jesus the fulfillment of his longing and exulted for joy (cf. Lk 2:22–38). This happened at an important moment in salvation history. For centuries the prophets had predicted the day when the Messiah would come to the Temple (e.g., Mal. 3:1). Jesus was forty days old, and was brought to Jerusalem by Joseph and Mary. The priest who was on duty that historic day, to receive the gifts for the redemption of the first-born son (cf. Ex. 13:11–14) and for the purification of the mother, was quite familiar with the Scripture; he probably even knew it by heart. Nonetheless, he did not notice that at that moment the prophecies were fulfilled. Of course, it happened in a way entirely different from how people had imagined. "My thoughts are not your thoughts, nor are your ways my ways—says the LORD" (Is 55:8).

Anyone whose images of God are too specific can easily miss the encounter with him, because God comes in a shape different from the one we expect. But two old people, who belonged to the *anawim*, to the Lord's poor, recognized the Messiah in the child. Simeon asks Mary to be allowed to take the child into his arms. In his joy he sings a song. We repeat it every day at Compline. The old man thinks universally. He sees in the child the glory for the people of Israel, but beyond that he also sees the light for the gentiles and the salvation of all nations. At the same time he personally experiences the fulfillment of his life, which he now can give back to God in complete peace. Together with him the aged widow Anna praises God. She spoke "about the child to all who were looking for the redemption of Jerusalem" (Lk 2:38).

But Simeon also bears witness that "This child is destined . . . to be a sign that will be opposed, so that the inner thoughts of many will be revealed" (Lk 2:34–35). The child presents us with an inescapable decision: for him or against him, as later he himself several times demands: "Whoever is not with me is against me" (Lk 11:23). It is noteworthy that Jesus also, and more than once, says exactly the opposite: "Whoever is not against you is for you" (Lk 9:50). That might sound like a contradiction. But the generous latter formulations always use the plural, and thus are meant for the community, whereas the "intolerant" version is in each case in the singular, and hence refers to the person of Jesus.

As a young man of twenty-two, Rembrandt painted this scene of Jesus' presentation in the Temple. At the end of his life, even as he had grown old and gray, he returned to the same episode, so as to express once again, in the last painting of his splendid career, the bright joy and the deep satisfaction of this encounter with Jesus, and thus to lay his life in God's hand. "As for me, I shall behold your face in righteousness; when I awake I shall be satisfied, beholding your likeness" (Ps 17:15).

The gospels repeatedly announce that in Jesus we find God's plenitude. The multiplication of the loaves and the marriage feast of Cana point to this. Jesus gives out bread and wine in abundance, and we are still living from them, in every celebration of the Eucharist. He surprises Peter and his companions with an overwhelming catch of fish, so that the glory of Jesus dawns on the fisherman from Galilee, who falls at Jesus' feet with the words: "Go away from me, Lord, for I am a sinful man!" (Lk 5:8). That doesn't mean that he quickly examined his conscience and so became aware of some sins he had committed, but rather that he experienced in Jesus the sublimity and fullness of God and with it his own unworthiness. In a similar fashion, the prophet Isaiah cries out in the vision of his calling: "Woe is me! I am lost, for I am a man of unclean lips, and I live among a people of unclean lips, yet my eyes have seen the king, the LORD of hosts" (Is 6:5).

John's gospel often stresses emphatically the glory of God in Jesus. This divine glory, which according to the Old Testament no human being can look upon and live, is visible in Jesus: "We have seen his glory, the glory as of the Father's only Son, full of grace and truth. . . . From his fullness we have all received, grace upon grace" (Jn 1:14, 16).

In the New Testament, above all in the Pauline letters, there are well over one hundred names and images for Jesus. The first Christians found in him such a fullness that language didn't suffice to express it all. This experience made the believers—they called themselves "saints"—happy and free. The more fulfilled a life people live, the more easily they can let go. Their hands don't need to cling feverishly to what has come their way. Fulfilled people can open themselves in trust and inner freedom. They can enjoy things the way people who are not free cannot. And they can renounce some things. When the time comes, they can, like Simeon, lay down their lives in peace.

It is important that we live in the center of the glad tidings and not on the margin. Those who continually busy themselves with the question if this or that can still be made to jibe with the gospel, or perhaps no longer can, are living close to the frontier; or have already crossed over it and they are missing the true experience that Jesus wants to impart. These Christians aren't really free and happy. They are too intent on their own profit and advantage, always busy with the issue of "What do I get out of it?" But this attitude only minimizes the glad tidings, and so they cannot be lived and enjoyed to the fullest. Saint Paul warns: "The point is this: the one who sows sparingly will also reap sparingly, and the one who sows bountifully will also reap bountifully" (2 Cor 9:6).

The gospels tell us that in life there is always a danger of mistaken priorities. The first and greatest commandment is and remains in the New Testament, as in the Old: "Hear, O Israel: The LORD is our God, the LORD alone. You shall love the LORD your God with all your heart, and with all your soul, and with all your might" (Dt 6:4–5). Jesus lived and proclaimed this with total dedication. Some of those who have committed themselves to this message and begun to live accordingly can lose, after a while, their radical orientation to God. Something else slips into the center, usually something that we have become involved with for God's sake and that we have taken on in his service. In the long run this Something becomes more important than God himself. Basically, a pious idol has set itself up in our life, perhaps without our even noticing it. We still pray to God, but only that he will bless our most important concern. Serving God has imperceptibly and unconsciously turned into making use of God. A certain egocentrism has crept in and taken over, conceding too much room to our own planning, our own satisfaction, our own prestige.

With British humor, C.S. Lewis tells how a good many preachers deliver their first sermons with great effort and all for God's glory; but after some time they find it so satisfying that they have a hard time stopping. Some years ago I lived with a mischievous member of my order who occasionally recounted at lunch that at morning mass, during the sermon, he had said a prayer to Saint Anthony (the patron of those who have lost something). The first time I didn't know what he meant; but the others knew already. He had prayed that the preacher would find the end of his sermon.

When God is no longer the center, life gets harder than it has to be. Brother Klaus von Flüe (1417–1487) had a vision of a well. It is rather complicated, but it has a painful and intimidating relevance. To put it briefly, Klaus sees in a village a large group of people who are doing hard work and yet remain very poor. He also sees a small building, which he walks into. He enters a kitchen that belongs to the whole community. As he climbs up "a little staircase, perhaps all of four steps," he discovers a chest, out of which "as quick as lightning shoots, with a mighty roar, a great stream of three things, namely wine, oil, and honey. This stream is crystal clear. And however powerfully it flowed out, the chest still remained filled to the very top." He cannot understand how the people can work so hard and yet be so poor and still not enter the kitchen." And he saw no one go into the kitchen to draw from the well."

A poem by Artur Kleemann fits in well with this vision by Brother Klaus and with the content of this chapter:

Each day the old fountain quietly pours
out its water, steady as it goes.
I wish I were like this fountain,
and could always pass on what is in me.

But, giving, giving, every single day,
Tell me, fountain, doesn't it get to be a
bother?
Then the fountain says to me
(his fellow-toiler):
"I am only a fountain, not a wellspring
It flows to me—I pass it on,
That makes my nature glad and gay."

Thus I live in the fountain's way,
I daily draw strength for life's journey,
and will always—happily—pass on
what the wellspring gives me to live.

Dear Lord,

Think through my mind,

until your ideas are my ideas too.

Love through my heart,

until your feelings are my feelings too.

Make decisions through my will,

until your will is my will too.

Speak through my lips,

until your words are my words too.

Give to me grace. Take from me doubt.

Prune me. Transform me.

You alone know what is good for me.

Be with me, around me, on the left of me,

on the right of me, behind me,

before me, above me, beneath me, within me,

until we are two no more. Amen.

—JEAN MAALOUF

SUMMARY

God blesses us with a fullness of life and love, which found its perfect embodiment in the person of Jesus and which from him flows to us. In him we find our fulfillment such as the world cannot give. Simeon is an expressive example. In order to share in this fullness one has to live in the center of the Good News and not at the fringes. Compromising causes great losses.

Isaiah 6:1-8

Isaiah 12:3

Luke 2:22-38

Luke 5:1-11

1 Corinthians 10:1-4

Colossians 1:13-20

1. Can I describe an experience when I felt overwhelmed by God's fullness?

2. How do I try to find the way to the heart of the gospel?

3. What draws me away from the center of my faith?

4. What kinds of conversations or discussions help me to deepen my faith and what do I find unhelpful in this respect?

5. How would I verbalize in a modern way the vision of Brother Klaus von Flüe?

Jesus' Suffering, Our Suffering

We sometimes call the suffering a person has to endure his or her "cross." We often do this without reflecting, but it has a deeper meaning. In using the word, we are making a connection between our suffering and the suffering of Jesus. It is worthwhile probing into this connection. We can do it from both sides.

We are present in Jesus' suffering.

Perhaps we can rediscover ourselves in Pilate. He was an educated Roman, an experienced administrator and diplomat; but he was not up to the encounter with Jesus. In his heart he was convinced that Jesus had been falsely

accused, that he was in fact completely innocent. Although Pilate had, as he himself said,
"power to release" Jesus, he could not get up
the courage to actually make use of this power
(Jn 19:10). One gets the impression that he
couldn't even decide not to make a decision.
He desperately looked for compromises, and
in the process he plunged from one cruel injustice into the next—still worse—injustice. For
Jesus this attitude was fateful. First, Pilate tried
to shift the decision to the Tetrarch Herod (Lk
23:6–11) and after that to the people, offering
them the choice between Jesus and Barabbas.
Then, as a concession to the aroused mob, he
had Jesus scourged, although he twice admit-
ted: "I find no case against him" (Jn 18:38;
19:6). Then he brought the scourged and thorn-
crowned Jesus before the people in hopes that
now the bloodthirsty crowd would be satisfied. When they still refused to quiet down, he
gave in again, this time by issuing the brutal
sentence of death on the cross. Then he had the
nerve to wash his hands in the sight of the
crowd, saying, "I am innocent of this man's
blood" (Mt 27:24). He was definitively not!
How did Jesus experience this evident and
massive injustice? What did his heart feel?

Because Jesus is the Son of God, compromises in dealing with him are always dishonest.

The God of Our Deepest Longings

That would mean assigning to him a limited worth and de facto denying his divinity. The Son of God is the only one who may and must make the enormous claim that, "Whoever is not with me is against me" (Mt 12:30). Pilate experienced this in an infinitely tragic fashion. Precisely because the consequences of his half-heartedness were so cruel, he serves as a mirror for us in which we can clearly recognize our own wretched cowardice.

Apart from Pilate, many others play a role in the passion of Jesus, and to a certain extent we can perhaps identify with some of them. Judas has become the supreme instance of betrayal. He committed the monstrous act of betraying Jesus to his enemies with a kiss. The dimensions of his deed may well be beyond us. But Peter also betrayed Jesus, though on a smaller scale. For that very reason he is somewhat closer to us. Luke reports that after being taken prisoner, Jesus was led away to the house of the high priest. Then he adds the brief verse: "But Peter was following at a distance" (Lk 22:54). The fact that Peter kept his distance was likely connected to his refusal of suffering. Following Jesus demands the whole person; one cannot follow Jesus by halves. This had already led to painful conflict with Jesus much earlier. Immediately after Peter's grand confession:

"You are the Messiah, the son of the living God" (Mt 16:16), Jesus began to prepare his disciples for his suffering, which undeniably had to come. That provoked massive resistance from Peter: "'This must never happen to you!' But he [Jesus] turned and said to Peter: 'Get behind me, Satan! You are a stumbling block to me; for you are setting your mind not on divine things but on human things'" (Mt 16:22–23). For us Peter could be a good and sympathetic teacher, who makes us see that we have to give ourselves up to Jesus without reservation and without compromise.

Many people will recognize themselves in Simon of Cyrene, the man who was forced to carry Jesus' cross. He didn't want to, but he had no other choice. How did he feel about it? How did he perform his compulsory service? Did he sense anything of the spirit animating Jesus? In retrospect, was he grateful and happy that he could offer this help to the dying master and be so close—and, in a sense, so much like him—on the way of the cross? Is he a model and a help to us?

Veronica is not mentioned in the gospels. Tradition claims that she had the courage to defy the hostility and shame and do a small, loving service to Jesus—to wipe his face. The Lord is supposed to have richly rewarded her by imprinting the true image (which is what "Veronica" means) of his face on her veil. Do we find the courage to show our love to our Lord, even when we are mocked by those around us? Can we simply do it out of unguarded love for Jesus?

When Jesus was nailed to the cross, he prayed: "Father forgive them; for they do not know what they are doing" (Lk 23:34). This request doesn't just apply to the executioner's servants, who in fact didn't know what they were doing, and not just to the ones who gave the orders, who in their blindness couldn't see what they were up to; it applies to all of us. It is good to listen to these words of Jesus occasionally and to mull them over. Let them penetrate deeply into our hearts. From them we can draw the strength to forgive those who have done us wrong. Forgiving is an extremely hard and at the same time a supremely important art. The crucified Lord is our best teacher here.

Along with Jesus two criminals were crucified, one on his right, one on his left. They had walked with him on the utterly horrible way of the cross, and thus had after a fashion gotten to know him. One of them scorned the supposed Messiah. By contrast, the other one prayed: "Jesus, remember me when you come into your kingdom" (Lk 23:42). This is actually the one time in the four gospels that Jesus is addressed only by his name, without any further addition. The two criminals reacted in a fundamentally different way to Jesus' person and suffering. He is the "sign that will be opposed" (Lk 2:34). Do I sense a similar dichotomy going on in me? Do I rediscover myself in the suffering of Jesus?

Mary Magdalene stayed with Jesus through all the phases of his suffering, all the way to the cross. Amid unspeakable pain and with unshakable loyalty, she shared in Jesus' suffering, even as on Easter morning she didn't budge from the empty grave. Alongside her stood Jesus' mother (Jn 19:25–27). With her we too find our place in the passion, for as his final legacy, Jesus entrusts us to his mother and his mother to us. John, the only evangelist who mentions this, speaks here of the "disciple whom Jesus loved," without mentioning his name. This is usually taken as referring to John himself. But it applies to each one of us without exception, because we are all disciples whom Jesus loves. Under the cross Mary becomes our mother. We are all "predestined to be conformed to the image of his [God's] Son" (cf. Rom 8:29). This doesn't work without Mary. Thus we are all invited to take her to ourselves, as John did before us.

To be sure, there are in Jesus' passion other persons to whom we are connected. The Roman captain closely observed Jesus' entire Passion, because it took place under his direction. After the death of Jesus, with startling words that he himself likely didn't fathom, he cried out: "Truly this man was God's Son!" (Mk 15:39). We make this profession of faith together with him.

In the oldest creed Saint Paul states: "For I handed on to you as of first importance what I in turn had received: that Christ died for our sins in accordance with the scriptures" (1 Cor 15:3). This does not mean—as some Christians unfortunately think—that the Father had to be reconciled through the death of his Son on the cross, but rather that *we* had to be reconciled by it. In the New Testament, reconciliation never means that *God* is reconciled, but always that *human beings* are reconciled. Paul lays special stress on this: "All this is from God, who reconciled us to himself through Christ, and has given us the ministry of reconciliation; that is, in Christ God was reconciling the world to himself, not counting their trespasses against them, and entrusting the message of reconciliation to us" (2 Cor 5:18–19).

In the expression "Christ died for our sins," the word "for" (Greek *hyper*) has a triple meaning. First, "for our benefit": Jesus' death achieved reconciliation, the forgiveness of our guilt, to our advantage. Second, "for our sake": Jesus suffered from our guilt, whose forgiveness we ourselves could not accomplish. Third, "in our place": in his baptism Jesus established a solidarity with us sinful human beings to the extent that he took our guilt upon him. After an incubation period of three years he became, as it were, all "sin," and died in our place from this sickness of the soul that by nature was wholly alien to him (cf. 2 Cor 5:21). All the sins of all humanity literally hurt the Son of God. As our representative, he bore this suffering and died from it. That does not mean that he spared us the death we have to die, but that we die this death in communion with him and are led through it to salvation.

Jesus is present in our suffering.

Jesus didn't come to explain the mystery of suffering to us, to reveal its meaning to our rational mind. Even after his death, suffering remains a mystery, perhaps even more than it was before. He came to fill our suffering up to the brim with his presence and so to transform it into a path that it makes sense to take, because he takes it with us. We are allowed to share our suffering with him. Together with him we can say over and over again: "Father, into your hands I commend my spirit" (Lk 23:46; cf. Ps 31:5).

Suffering is always, in and of itself, meaningless. On its own terms it is destructive and absurd. It acquires meaning only when a person manages to give the suffering meaning. Unfortunately, many people are not able to do this. In that case the suffering remains sterile and can lead to egocentrism and bitterness. In everyday situations and, still more, in difficult decisions this attitude can have negative effects and lead to false choices. No human being has ever given a deeper meaning to his or her suffering than Jesus did on the cross. "Taking up one's cross" means accepting one's suffering and, in the spirit of Jesus and through Jesus, arriving at a meaning for it.

Still, we first have to ask ourselves some questions, so that we don't stumble into a false, unbiblical spirituality of suffering and prematurely dodge our own responsibility. So, first of all, I have to ask whether or not it may in fact correspond to God's will that I change the situation that makes me suffer—or at least try to do this to the best of my ability. I also have to concretely ask myself whether the experience of suffering has something to do with my own behavior or my life-story, whether I should first ask the Lord to heal these wounds, and whether I myself shouldn't seek the help I need. Only then can I accept whatever "irreducible leftover" remains and in good conscience unite it with the cross of Jesus and bear it together with him.

Looking to the cross doesn't make the pain or suffering diminish, but now I am no longer alone: "And remember, I am with you always, to the end of the age" (Mt 28:20). We can pray with Rabindranath Tagore: "Grant that I not be a coward who recognizes your grace only in success." Jesus unmistakably declared that no one can be his disciple without taking up one's cross and following him (cf. Lk 14:27, among other passages). The suffering that we take on in union with Jesus can heal us and cleanse us. Many people have grown through suffering shared with Jesus and have been led more deeply into the mystery of God's unfathomable love. Faith in the presence of the risen Lord gives our suffering a perspective, here in this life and beyond death.

I can look to Jesus in his suffering and open to him the feelings of my suffering. This is my Gethsemani, no doubt incomparably milder than his, but nevertheless extraordinarily harsh and difficult for me. Sufferings cannot be compared! I may ask the Lord to abide with me

The God of Our Deepest Longings

and watch with me. He will show himself to be more reliable and loyal than his disciples did.

We belong to the Lord, even in our suffering. Accompanying anyone on the path of suffering is an enormous challenge. There is no room here for ambiguities or half-truths, for flattery or commonplaces. We are challenged completely, and everything is demanded of us. At times this is precisely what makes it a great grace. Jesus goes with us on the path of our suffering: "Listen! I am standing at the door, knocking: if you hear my voice and open the door, I will come in to you and eat with you, and you with me" (Rev 3:20). In this way our personal Eucharist is carried out. In its transformation we too are transformed (cf. Jn 17:19).

While living in Berlin, Germany, I regularly visited a Sister in her forties who was dying from cancer of the liver. Of course, I always asked how she was doing; she would honestly and clearly speak about her pain and hardships, but after a fairly short time she would close this topic. The suffering was never denied or repressed, but there was more she wanted to share. In the midst of all anxieties and discomfort, there was the earnest will to surrender and with it a peace which surpasses our own doing and even our own understanding. It was hard for me to be confronted with the illness that was undoubtedly lethal, and yet God was present and close in an extraordinary way. I cannot explain it, not even express it in words, but after more than 20 years I still often think of those visits and remember them with deep gratitude and a sense of wonder. I hope and expect that many readers will understand what I am trying to say because they have had similar experiences.

A simple image may round out these thoughts: Our suffering is like a brook, perhaps a rather large one; but the suffering of Jesus is like a river. If we succeed in getting our brook to feed into the river of Jesus' passion, then we are saved. In that way our hardships are indissolubly taken up in his suffering. We can no longer dwell on our suffering without also being with him in his suffering. Together with his suffering our suffering too flows toward resurrection. That's not a theory, but, one hopes, a personal experience. Thanks be to him.

Gracious God,

You revealed yourself in the Old Testament

in unspeakable power and might,

but in the fullness of time even more

in the coming of your only begotten Son among us.

He showed us his love to the very end,

most of all in the holy Eucharist

and in his passion and death.

We ask you that we may understand

your first and last word in him

and that we may experience his presence among us

in good and bad days until the end of time. Amen.

SUMMARY

The passion of Jesus and our own sufferings are mysteriously and blessedly connected. We are present in Jesus' sufferings. It is salutary to identify with various people who play a role in the passion of Jesus, and to realize that Jesus died for us. Jesus is also present in our sufferings, as he promised in his last words in Matthew's gospel. This can be a source of strength and peace. We touch here upon the mystery this booklet deals with. We cannot grasp it but we can find our home in it.

The God of Our Deepest Longings

SCRIPTURE PASSAGES

Isaiah 52:13-53:12

Luke 23:26-46

2 Corinthians 4:7-11; 12:10

Colossians 1:24

1. With which characters in the passion of Jesus can I identify and why?

2. In what way is the passion of Jesus a challenge and perhaps a scandal to me?

3. How do I see the place of the Father in the passion of his Son?

4. Have I ever, either in myself or in others, witnessed an inexplicable peace in the midst of suffering?

Shalom

Those who truly want to make their home in the Mystery will be confronted with their fears. That is to be expected and healthy because we all have a natural desire to have things under control, and it is an essential feature of Mystery that we do not have it in our grip. This demands a great deal of trust and a complete surrender. Many feelings and forces within us fight against it. We have never seen God and we are even told that God is a consuming fire (cf. Dt 4:24; Is 33:14; Heb 12:29). God is awesome and, yes, to be feared.

The Hebrew word *yare* is usually translated as "fear." It is, however, important to realize that this "fear" can have two quite different meanings. When said in relation to God, it has a thoroughly positive significance. Fear of God is awe, deep respect, great reverence. Fear of God and love of God are intimately connected and even mentioned in one breath: "So now, Israel, what does the LORD your God require of you? Only to fear the LORD your God, to walk in his ways, to love him, to serve the LORD your God with all your heart and with all your soul" (Dt 10:12). The fear of God is a precious and highly praised quality. It is called a splendid crown, the beginning and root and fullness of wisdom. It makes health and salvation spring forth and grants us a long life (cf. Sir 1:11–20).

When the word *yare* is used in human relations it has a decidedly different meaning, namely that of being afraid, of dread and anxiety. This kind of fear is in some ways necessary. Those who never see danger are dangerous people and those who never feel fear in the face of dangers are not, as a rule, up to confronting those dangers. An appropriate degree of fear is necessary for recognizing danger and avoiding it by flight or by some other response. But fear can easily become a huge obstacle in the lives of many people. The Bible warns us often (it is said 365 times): "Fear not." In the gospels Jesus repeats this caution more than ninety times. It is obvious that Jesus

The God of Our Deepest Longings

considered it as an important part of his mission to set us free from unhealthy fear.

In point of fact, fear often has negative effects on us. It narrows, hardens, and cripples. It makes breathing harder and causes palpitations of the heart. It prevents us from hearing correctly, distorts our perception, stops us from speaking out when something is wrong, and often tempts us to simply look the other way. It blocks contacts and causes us to misinterpret words and gestures. It occasionally seduces us into fleeing forward, disguising this flight as courage. It not only closes doors, but hearts and institutions as well. I'm convinced that a great deal of lovelessness arises not so much out of malice as out of inappropriate fear. In our society, often characterized by constant social noise, we find many people who are afraid of silence, of encountering themselves, and above all of standing before God. Television, iPods, and cell phones make such escape easy, sometimes too easy. Still more profound is the fear of realizing oneself and making the most of one's talents. In the parable of the talents, the servant who buried his talent in the ground is sharply blamed and punished in the parable as a "wicked and lazy slave" (Mt 25:26–30). In contrast, Jesus tell us: "My Father is glorified by this, that you bear much fruit and become my disciples" (Jn 15:8). Become who you are! In so doing you glorify God. The secret to achieving this is revealed in the next verse: "As the Father loves me, so I love you. Remain in my love" (Jn 15:9). Be at home in the Mystery!

Writer and member of the Catholic resistance in Nazi-Germany Reinhold Schneider (1903–1958) experienced the kind of fear that makes us sick both in himself and all around him. Hence he could credibly write: "The power, the kingdom of evil is based on fear. That is why the Evil One increases and spreads fear wherever he wishes to found and maintain his empire. He can't extend his frontiers any farther than fear." Fears that keep us apart from God, our fellow men and women, and ourselves can be overcome only by bravely confronting them. That is exactly what Jesus encourages us to do. The greater our fear of God, the better equipped we are to overcome our negative fears.

The first Easter evening as described in the Gospel of John (20:19–23) was a paradoxical affair. It was the greatest day in salvation history, the day on which Jesus overcame death, "the last enemy," when the Father, in his transcendent fidelity, raised up his Son Jesus from the grave to a new life where "death no longer has dominion over him" (Rom 6:9). It is the day of an unimaginably deep and all-embracing joy. Nevertheless, out of fear of the Jews, Jesus' disciples huddled behind closed doors, locked in. They let themselves be ruled and cramped by the fear that Jesus had always warned them against. They displayed a behavior that was the total opposite of the example and teaching of Jesus, and thereby bitterly disappointed their master. But the risen Lord didn't reproach them. It strikes us that after his resurrection Jesus didn't have a word of blame for anyone, although he really had reason to. No, Jesus didn't think it beneath him to walk—even through closed doors—right into all this fear, which he did not want at all. It is comforting to know that Jesus is also in the midst of our fear, as he will be in the midst of our death—Jesus, the faithful one!

His greeting is: Shalom! Even today this is the normal Jewish greeting. The word *shalom* means more than our word "peace." It expresses harmony in every sense: between God and humanity, between body and soul, between individual persons, between nations, between a person and the world around him or her. Shalom includes justice, in keeping with the important and oft-repeated motto of Pope John Paul II: "No peace without justice, no justice without forgiveness." In the mouth of the risen

Lord, shalom has still a richer content: It means that peace which the world can neither give nor take away. The risen Jesus *is* himself this peace (cf. Eph 2:14). He bears in himself the force that breaks down barriers, that tears up everything that narrows and separates us. "As many of you as were baptized into Christ have clothed yourselves with Christ. There is no longer Jew or Greek, there is no longer slave or free, there is no longer male and female; for all of you are one in Christ Jesus" (Gal 3:27–28).

After this greeting Jesus showed his disciples the marks of the wounds in his hands and in his side. They are the traces of suffering that are forever engraved in the glorified body of the Risen One. Some day we too will see them! From now on these wounds are the proof of his identity. They are the permanent signs of his love that go all the way. They show the unbroken connection between suffering and resurrection, which belongs to the core of our faith and which Jesus himself has described in the simple and very convincing image of the grain of wheat: "Very truly, I tell you, unless a grain of wheat falls into the earth and dies, it remains just a single grain; but if it dies, it bears much fruit" (Jn 12:24).

"Then the disciples rejoiced." During his public life what Jesus always had in mind was giving us perfect joy (cf. Jn 15:11; 16:24; 17:13). For this reason Jesus' message is called "glad tidings." Now that joy breaks through, even if at first only in a preliminary manner. Ignatius has the retreatant pray for the grace of an intense joy over the ever-so-great glory and joy of Christ, our Lord (*Sp Ex* 221). So we ask for a selfless joy, simply a joy over Jesus' joy. The popular saying has it that we find out who our true friends are in times of trouble. That is doubtlessly true. But Hassidism completes this truth by teaching that we get to know our true friends in times of joy and success. This may actually contain a deeper truth. Genuine friends are those who truly and unselfishly rejoice in the good fortunes of others rather than experience feelings of jealousy or greed for profit. In both senses we want to be true friends of Jesus. That is why Ignatius has us pray for this joy.

After Jesus has once again wished peace, he makes a pointed remark: "As my Father has sent me, so I send you" (Jn 20:21). He passes on his mission, from which and for which he lived, to his disciples. From now on he has only our hands and our feet, our mouth and our heart. A mission is always a matter of trust on both sides. Between Father and Son there was a complete and unqualified trust. God gives us, too, a magnanimous advance of trust. We are taken into the relationship between Father and Son. Every Christian is sent on a mission. That is an essential part of our baptism. God wants to work through us, and he wants to continue in us the mission of his Son. This mission gives our life precious meaning and incomparable value, and at the same time it liberates us from the fixation on our own strengths or weaknesses. The key to mission consists precisely in this: letting God work in and through us. "Now may the God of peace . . . make you complete in everything that is good so that you may do his will, working among us that which is pleasing in his sight, through Jesus Christ, to whom be glory forever" (Heb 13:20–21). That lifts a heavy weight off our shoulders. To entrust ourselves completely to God, however, calls for openness and inner freedom, which in turn demands an ongoing conversion. It is precisely in one's mission that one can cling to non-essentials, which gradually take on too much value. Actually, we have to take on our mission anew every day, so that we don't hijack it for our own goals, because then it would no longer be a mission.

In John 15:9 Jesus says: "As the Father has loved me, so I have loved you." Except for a single word, this remark is identical with the command of mission that we are considering here: "As the Father has sent me, so I have sent you." This shows us that love and mission are interchangeable, "love" meaning in the first place the love which God has for us, since that's what Jesus is talking about in this verse. "Mission" is the river bed of this love. Just as a river carves out a bed, without which it wouldn't be a river but merely a swamp, so the love of God builds a channel in us through which this love streams forth and so reaches other human beings. Here the being at home in the Mystery unfolds a dynamism none of us could have imagined. "Hope does not disappoint us, because God's love has been poured into our hearts through the Holy Spirit that has been given to us" (Rom 5:5). The love of God that Paul writes about here is once again first and foremost the love that God loves with. It is identical with the Holy Spirit who has been given to us. God's loving takes place in us, in its infinite dynamism and creativity.

I am often happily surprised that the Gospel is so simple. "God is love" may well be the most important message of the whole Bible. All we have to do is to open up to this love until it fills our hearts to the brim and, yes, until overflowing. In this way God's love flows through us to our fellow men and women, and so the whole law is fulfilled (cf. Rom 13:8–10). That is what it is all about.

Mission demands the dedication of our whole self, but is at the same time enormously freeing and liberating. The center of gravity is no longer me, but God working in and through me. Mission enables us to accomplish tasks that we could never master on our own. God knows our limits, heaven be praised, but God can also make us transcend our limits. I am sure many of us have experienced this in the service of the Lord. Indeed, God is full of surprises, always greater than we expect. The psalmist articulates this phenomenon praying: "He brought me out in a broad place . . . and by my God I can leap over a wall." (Ps 18:20, 30).

Jesus empowered the mission of his disciples with the ancient biblical sign of breathing on them and with the weighty comment: "Receive the Holy Spirit." This event is called the Johannine Pentecost, because apart from this there is no sending of the Spirit in John's gospel. Ten disciples were on hand, since Judas had taken his life and Thomas was not present that evening. We may join the disciples and receive the Holy Spirit and be sent forth with them. I like to imagine how Jesus went up to each one, looked on him with great warmth and trust, breathed powerfully on him, perhaps laid his hands on him and embraced him. Then he sent him forth in his name and in his Spirit. We naturally think of Genesis 2:7: "And then the LORD God formed man from the dust of the ground, and breathed into his nostrils the breath of life; and the man became a living being." Or we may recall the powerful vision of Ezekiel where the prophet saw a broad valley full of dead bones and received the command: "Prophesy to the breath. . . . Come from the four winds, O breath, and breathe upon these slain, that they may live." He spoke as he was bidden: "Thus says the LORD God . . . I will put my spirit within you, and you shall live, and I will place you on your own soil; then you shall know that I, the LORD, have spoken and will act" (Ez 37:9–14). On Easter evening this Spirit took fear away from the disciples, the fear that narrowed them and bottled them up. Then the Spirit drove them out to the ends of the earth, just as Jesus had predicted: "You will receive power when the Holy Spirit has come upon you; and you will be my witnesses in Jerusalem, in all Judea and Samaria, and to the ends of the earth" (Acts 1:8).

To conclude this encounter, Jesus gave his disciples the special gift of the authority to forgive sins: "Whose sins you forgive, are forgiven them" (Jn 20:23). Here we must not forget that both the scribes and Jesus are in agreement that no one but God can forgive sins (cf. Mk 2:7). Forgiving is the perfection of love. It is more than just repair work; instead it truly creates us anew, makes us new persons. This is something we are not capable of ourselves; it is exclusively in God's hands. The fact that Jesus forgives sins is explicit evidence of his unity with the Father. Now he entrusts this divine authority to his Church so that it can continue his mission even in this extremely delicate and important domain.

Death and guilt are liminal experiences that we cannot master with our own powers. For this reason they are generally shunned and even repressed. It is exactly at these two especially sensitive places that Jesus comes to meet us. The risen Lord has conquered death and gives, as an Easter present to his Church, the authority to forgive sins. The second half of verse 23 includes the refusal of forgiveness. The fact that this is mentioned might be a Jewish way of expressing the fullness of that authority; forgiving and the refusal to forgive constitute the unlimited authority of forgive- ness. In the resurrection and the forgiveness of sin God comes closest to us in meeting us precisely at the borderline situations of our

The God of Our Deepest Longings

human existence and helping us to move beyond these human limits into "the mystery that was kept secret for long ages" (Rom 16:25).

God of faithfulness and surprises,

you gave Jesus, our brother, life beyond death

and all power in heaven and on earth.

He shared his gifts with us

and chose us to continue his mission until the end of time.

He works through our hands,

he speaks with our tongue,

he loves with our heart.

Who are we, God,

that you have done such great things to us?

Never let us take for granted your generosity

nor become complacent in our good fortune.

Help us to become ever more transparent

for your life and your love

and thus to accomplish our mission

according to your most holy will.

S U M M A R Y

The risen Jesus steps through closed doors into
the midst of the fear that stifles his disciples. He
identifies himself by showing the scars of the cru-
cifixion. He brings peace and great joy. He
entrusts the disciples with the mission to continue
the mission which he himself received from his
Father. He breathes on them, so that the ruach
of the Lord, the Holy Spirit inspires them. As a
special Easter gift he confers on his church the
sacrament of reconciliation.

Jeremiah 1:4-10

Matthew 28:16-20

John 15:8-17

John 20:19-23

1 Corinthians 15:12-57

QUESTIONS FOR REFLECTION

1. What does the resurrection of Jesus mean to me personally?

2. What does it mean for me to believe in the resurrection of the dead?

3. How do I draw strength from my faith to overcome false fears?

4. In what way do I see my life as a continuation of the mission of Jesus?

5. What role has the sacrament of reconciliation played in my life, in the past and today?

Peter van Breemen, S.J., is author of several books, including *The God Who Won't Let Go* (Ave Maria Press, 2001) and *Summoned at Every Age* (Ave Maria Press, 2005), as well as *Bread That Is Broken, Called by Name, Certain as the Dawn,* and *Let All God's Glory Through.* He has been a member of the Jesuit order since 1945 and has worked extensively in novice and priest formation. His influence on the Church stretches worldwide with best-selling books published in many languages. He presently resides in Aachen, Germany, where he directs retreats and works as a spiritual director.